The Art of Dog Stewardship

NIPA® GENX ELECTRONIC RESOURCES & SOLUTIONS P. LTD.
New Delhi-110 034

About the Authors

Dr. Sanjib Borah is an esteemed academician and researcher, currently an Associate Professor in the Department of Veterinary Physiology and Biochemistry at Lakhimpur College of Veterinary Science, Assam Agricultural University. His research focuses on reproductive physiology and molecular biology in livestock, with notable work on growth, reproduction, stress and immune function. Proficient in Assisted Reproductive Techniques and molecular biology, he has secured substantial research funding from prestigious research funding agencies. These projects have not only advanced scientific knowledge but have also yielded practical implications for enhancing animal productivity and welfare. He was also a part of the research team to produce world's first Embryo Transfer Technology (ETT) born yak calf - MISMO in 2005. An accomplished educator since 2014, Dr. Borah has received multiple awards and authored numerous research papers, contributed to books and participated in scientific committees, making significant contributions to veterinary science and animal welfare.

Dr. Simson Soren, Ph.D. working as Assistant Professor in the Department of Veterinary Physiology and Biochemistry at Lakhimpur College of Veterinary Science, Assam Agricultural University, Joyhing, North Lakhimpur Since 2019. Dr. S. Soren awarded Ph.D. degree in the discipline of Animal Physiology from ICAR-NDRI, Karnal in the year 2016. A recipient of the certificate course held by FELASA (Federation of European Laboratory Animal Science Association) accredited course (FELASA Ref. 052/15) "In Laboratory Animal Sciences"Laboratory Animal Medicine, Centre for Animal Health Studies, TANUVAS, Chennai, India (2016). Recipient of the certificate of competence by School of Life Science, Jawaharlal Nehru University (JNU), New Delhi (2016) in handling and care of laboratory animals. He was awarded Master of Veterinary Science (Veterinary Physiology) in 2011 and Bachelor of Veterinary Science and Animal Husbandry from College of Veterinary Science, Assam Agricultural University, Khanapara, Guwahati (2008). He was also a part of the research team to produce world's first test tube Yak Calf named "NORGYAL". His research works have been recognised in various capacities at national and international platforms and actively published scientific articles, book chapters, and popular articles.

The Art of Dog Stewardship

Sanjib Borah
Associate Professor
Department of Veterinary Physiology and Biochemistry
Lakhimpur College of Veterinary Science
Assam Agricultural University, Assam

Simson Soren
Assistant Professor
Department of Veterinary Physiology and Biochemistry
Lakhimpur College of Veterinary Science
Assam Agricultural University, Assam

NIPA® GENX ELECTRONIC RESOURCES & SOLUTIONS P. LTD.
New Delhi-110 034

NIPA® GENX ELECTRONIC
RESOURCES & SOLUTIONS P. LTD.

101,103, Vikas Surya Plaza, CU Block
L.S.C. Market, Pitam Pura, New Delhi-110 034
Ph : +91-11-43860225, Mob.: +91 9717133558, 9540816132
E-mail: newindiapublishingagency@gmail.com
Website: www.nipaersources.com

Print ISBN: 978-93-58879-66-7

ebook ISBN: 978-93-58875-98-0

NIPA® also publishes books in a variety of electronic formats. Some content that appears in print may not be available in electronic books, and vice versa.

Composed and Designed by NIPA®.

Dedicated to My Parents

This book is dedicated to my loving parents

Mr. Chandra Kanta Borah and Mrs. Phul Borah

Your unwavering suopport, endless love, and
infinite wisdom have been the guiding light in my life.
I am forever grateful for your
Sacrifices and the vlaues you have instilled in me.

Preface

In recent years, pet ownership in India has seen a remarkable surge, with dogs becoming an integral part of countless households across the country. These loyal and affectionate companions bring immense joy and unwavering companionship to their families. However, the journey of raising and caring for a pet dog is not without its challenges. As a pet owner, ensuring the health, safety, and well-being of your canine friend requires a comprehensive understanding of various aspects of dog care.

This book has been meticulously compiled to serve as a definitive resource for both novice and seasoned dog owners. With the diverse climate, unique environmental factors, and distinct challenges that come with pet ownership in India, this guide aims to provide tailored advice and practical solutions for every aspect of canine care.

The chapters within this book cover a wide array of topics, each crucial to the holistic well-being of your pet dog. Each chapter is designed to provide in-depth knowledge, practical tips, and expert advice to ensure your pet dog leads a healthy, happy, and fulfilling life. Whether you are considering bringing a new puppy into your home, caring for a senior dog, or looking for ways to enhance your pet's daily routine, this book is your ultimate companion in the rewarding journey of pet dog ownership.

We hope that this guide will not only help you in providing the best care for your beloved pet but also deepen the bond you share with your furry friend. Happy reading and happy pet parenting!

June 2024

Sanjib Borah
Simson Soren

Contents

Preface .... *vii*

1. Finding the Perfect Canine Companion: Suitable Dog Breeds for Pets in India 1
2. Keep Your Furry Companion Cool and Safe in Summer 15
3. Springtime Care Tips for Your Beloved Canine Companion 19
4. Winter Care Guide: Keeping Your Furry Friend Safe and Cozy 21
5. Common Diseases in Pet Dogs and Prevention Measures: A Comprehensive Guide 23
6. A Guide to Skin Care and Management for Your Pet Dog 27
7. Essential Eye and Ear Care: Maintaining Your Pet Dog's Sensory Health 31
8. Understanding Normal Behavior in Pet Dogs: A Guide for Pet Owners 33
9. Exercise Guide for Dogs 37
10. Oral Care for Pet Dogs: An In-Depth Guide 41
11. Care and Management of Dogs During Travel: A Comprehensive Guide 45
12. Caring for Senior Dogs: Health and Comfort 49
13. Care Management of Dogs During Pregnancy and Whelping 53
14. Grooming and Hygiene of Pet Dogs 57
15. Reduce the Risk to Pet-Associated Zoonotic Infections 61
16. Care for your Dog During a Disaster 65
17. Vaccination Schedule for Dogs: A Comprehensive Guide 69
18. Nutritional Guide for Pet Dogs of Different Age Groups 75

Index 79

1

Finding the Perfect Canine Companion Suitable Dog Breeds for Pets in India

Common Exotic and Indian Dog Breeds

India is home to a rich diversity of dog breeds both indigenous and exotic, each with unique traits suited to different environments and lifestyles. Among the exotic dog breeds that have gained popularity in India are the Labrador retriever, Golden Retriever, Beagle and German shepherd. These breeds often imported and are known for their friendly nature, intelligence and trainability. Labradors and Golden Retrievers are particularly famous for their loyalty and gentleness, making them excellent family pets. The Beagle, with its keen sense of smell and compact size, is a favourite among urban dwellers, while the German shepherd is valued for its protective instincts and versatility in roles like police work, guard duties and service tasks.

In contrast, Indian dog breeds, many of which are lesser-known globally, are uniquely adapted to the country's diverse climate and conditions. The Indian Pariah Dog is one of the oldest and most resilient breeds, found naturally across the country. Known for its strong immune system, minimal grooming needs and intelligence, the Indian Pariah is an exceptional companion that thrives with minimal human intervention. Another indigenous breed is the Rajapalayam, a sighthound from Tamil Nadu, historically used for hunting boar and protecting livestock. With its striking white coat and regal demeanour, the Rajapalayam is revered for its loyalty and bravery. The Mudhol Hound/ Caravan Hound, from the Deccan Plateau region (Andhra Pradesh, Karnataka, Maharashtra, Telangana and Tamil Nadu of India), is another notable Indian breed, known for its speed, agility and endurance, often used in hunting and guarding. Chippiparai, another hound from Tamil Nadu, has a sleek body designed for speed and was historically favoured by royalty for hunting small game. The Kanni, also native to Tamil Nadu, is a close relative of the Chippiparai and is recognized for its grace and loyalty, often kept as a companion dog.

While these Indian breeds may not be as globally recognized as their exotic counterparts, they are well-suited to the Indian climate and lifestyle.

Additionally, many animal welfare advocates in India promote the adoption of indigenous breeds due to their adaptability, resilience to disease and the ease of care compared to some exotic breeds, which may face challenges like heat sensitivity and dietary restrictions in the Indian environment.

The rising awareness of indigenous dog breeds and their advantages has led to an increasing interest in preserving and promoting these breeds in India. However, exotic breeds continue to dominate urban households, primarily due to their international appeal and perceived status symbols. Nonetheless, both exotic and Indian breeds can thrive when given proper care, love, and attention, making them valuable companions for families across the country.

The following table describes the origin and suitable environment of some common breeds of dog

COMMON EXOTIC BREEDS OF DOG			
S. No.	**Dog Breeds**	**Origin**	**Environment**
1	 **German Shepherd**	Germany	German Shepherds are adaptable to various temperatures, but they thrive best in temperatures between 50°F (10°C) and 80°F (27°C).
2	 **Saint Bernard**	Switzerland	St. Bernards are typically comfortable in temperatures as low as 20°F to 45°F (-6°C to 7°C). limited heat tolerance
3	 Labrador Retriever	Newfound land	Ideal Environment/ Temperature: 10° to 26°C.

4	 **Newfoundland**	Newfound-land Land, Canada	Newfies can comfortably tolerate temperatures between 10F to 80F.
5	 **Siberian Husky**	Siberia	It is able to withstand temperatures as low as −50 to −60 °C (−58 to −76 °F).
6	 **Samoyed**	Russia	Not ideally suited for hot climates, around 75 degrees may be best.
7	 **Akita**	Japan	Akitas have low tolerance to heat. They are most comfortable in mild weather, ranging from 24 to 30 degrees Celsius.

8	 **Bernese Mountain Dog**	Switzerland	The breed was developed by the Swiss to live in the Alps where temperatures rarely reach 75°, even in the hottest months. Most Bernese Mountain Dogs love cold weather and snow
9	 **Tibetan Mastiff**	Tibet	Tibetan mastiff is used to live in extremely harsh climate condition, where degrees can deeply fall below 0°C (32°F) for a lot of months.
10	 **Norwegian Elkhound**	Norway	Given its origins, the Norwegian Elkhound has excellent tolerance for cold, even arctic temperatures. On the other hand, the Norwegian Elkhound has very low tolerance for heat. Anything above 75 or 80 degrees is not great for this dog
11	 **Finnish Spitz**	Finland	Aim for a home environment that's consistently between 60 to 70 degrees Fahrenheit.

12	 **Scottish Terrier**	Scotland	Their ideal comfortable range is between 15 Degree Celcius and 25 degree celcius, they feel most comfortable at this range .
13	 **Beagle**	Great Britain	Mild to cool temperatures can be enjoyable for a Beagle,temperatures below 32°F (0°C) can start to pose risks, especially if the dog is exposed for prolonged periods.
14	 **Poodle**	Great Britain	Poodle-dog bush is native to temperate environments where the temperature generally fluctuates between 50 to 95 °F (10 to 35 °C). It prefers warmer weather.
15	 **Chihuahua**	Mexico	A comfortable indoor temperature for a Chihuahua is around 68-72°F (20-22°C).

16	 **Dachshund**	Germany	The comfortable indoor temperature for a Dachshund in winter is around 68-72°F (20-22°C).
17	 **Rottweiler**	Germany	Rottweiler out to play in cold weather. However, the temperatures, should not fall below 40 degrees. Anything below 20 degrees is downright dangerous for your Rottweiler.
18	 **Border Collies**	Scotland	Border Collies are generally well-suited to colder climates. They tend to be comfortable between 30°F to 70°F (-1°C to 21°C)
19	 **Great Dane**	Germany	Any temperature above 30–32 degrees and the same humidity will is considered bad for the dog .Great Danes are sensitive to frigid temperatures

20	 **Boxer**	Germany	Boxers do not handle cold or extreme heat at all. Ideal indoor temperature for a Boxer ranges from 68°F to 72°F (20°C – 22°C). This range is comfortable for them,
21	 **Maltese Dog**	Malta	Most Maltese do not tolerate cold weather well because of their lack of undercoat and small size.
22	 **Pomeranian**	Germany	The ideal indoor temperature for Pomeranians in winter should be comfortable and warm, typically around 68-72°F (20-22°C). This range helps them maintain their body heat and stay comfortable during colder months.
23	 **American Eskimo Dog**	Germany	Colder temperatures, 32 and under would be good, but not too cold as -50 degrees. Eskies are built for snow and cold, but they can handle hot weather with considerations. The Eskie's fluffy coat insulates him against hot weather and shouldn't be shaved in the summer. And while some hot weather is fine for Eskies, extreme temperatures may be too much for this cool-weather-loving breed.

24	 **Shih Tzu**	Tibet	The ideal indoor temperature for a Shih Tzu is between 68°F and 78°F (20°C – 25°C). This range keeps them comfortable without overheating or getting too cold, especially given their susceptibility to respiratory issues.
25	 **Doberman**	Germany	They prefer temperatures that are not too hot or too cold, typically ranging from 50°F to 70°F (10°C to 21°C).
26	 **American Bully**	United States	Bulldogs can overheat quickly, even in temperatures of 85 degrees Fahrenheit. Their shorter muzzles make it harder to release extra heat by panting, so the excess heat can take its toll quickly
27	 **Yorkshire Terrier**	England	The ideal indoor temperature for a Yorkie ranges from 68°F to 72°F (20°C to 22°C).

28	 **Alaskan Malamute**	Alaska	Alaskan Malamutes are bred for cold weather and have a double coat that insulates them from the cold.
29	 **Airedale Terrier**	Yorkshire, England	The Airedale Terrier does well in cold weather. Airedales thrive in hot weather. The short and wiry hair on the bodies allows them to tolerate extremely hot temperatures.
30	 **Bull Terrier**	England	When the temperature drops to around 45°F/7°C, Bull Terriers start feeling uncomfortable. The dogs do well in hot weather but tend to be more sensitive to colder weather conditions.
31	 **English Cocker Spaniel**	Spain	Cocker Spaniels are best suited to moderate climates. They can adapt to a range of temperatures, but extreme heat or cold can pose challenges. Any temperature above 30–32 degrees and the same humidity will be very bad deal for the dog

32	 **Dalmatian**	Crotia	Dalmatians have a short coat that is well-suited to warmer climates. They can handle heat better than many long-haired breeds.

COMMON INDIAN BREEDS OF DOG			
S. No.	**Dog Breeds**	**Origin**	**Environment**
1	 **Chippiparai**	Tamil Nadu	Chippiparai dogs originated in the hot environment of southern India, acquiring a short, silky coat that helps them stay cool.
2	 **Jonangi**	Andhra Pradesh	Jonangi dogs have very short coats to withstand the scorching Indian temperatures.

<table>
<tr><td>3</td><td>
Mudhol Hound</td><td>North Karnataka's Bagalkote and Vijaypura districts</td><td>It is happiest outdoors, and is at home in tropical climates.</td></tr>
<tr><td>4</td><td>
Kombai dog</td><td>Tamil Nadu</td><td>The intense heat of southern India has indeed been adapted by Kombai Dogs. In hot weather, they should have access to shade and water.</td></tr>
<tr><td>5</td><td>
Gaddi Kutta</td><td>The Himalayan foothills from eastern Nepal to Kashmir</td><td>Gaddi Dog Can't Live Inhot Climate. Gaddi dogs are native to the cold regions of the Himalayas, which are not suitable for living in areas with hot climates.</td></tr>
<tr><td>6</td><td>
Rajapalayam Hound</td><td>Tamil Nadu</td><td>They are not suited for winter weather and cold climates.</td></tr>
<tr><td>7</td><td>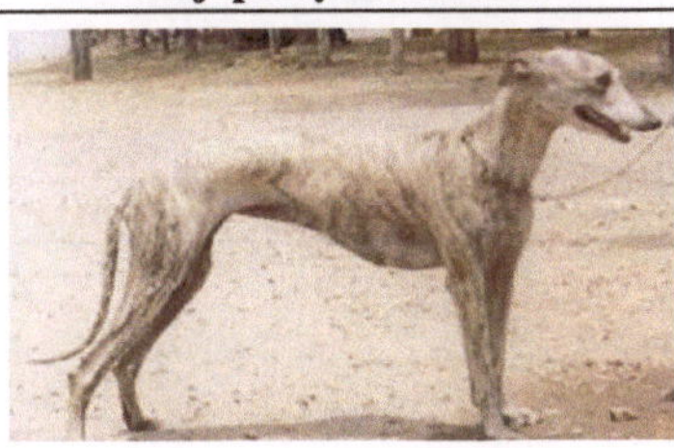
Rampur Greyhound</td><td>Rampur</td><td>They are quite comfortable in hot weather conditions and require no special treatment.</td></tr>
</table>

8	 **Indian pariah dog**	Sindh region of Pakistan	These dogs can withstand extreme temperatures, from the intense heat of summer to the cooler winters in various parts of the country.
9	 **Kanni**	Tamil Nadu	Kannis live in a temperate climate zone.
10	 **Kaikadi**	Maharashtra and parts of Gujarat	Kaikadi dogs are not recommended to live in extream cold weather.
11	 **Bakharwal dog**	Jammu and Kashmir	Bakharwal Dogs can tolerate temperatures ranging from hot (up to 35°C) to cold (down to -5°C)

Suitable Dog Breeds in the climatic condition of India

Choosing a dog breed that suits your lifestyle and environment is crucial for a harmonious relationship between pet and owner. In India, where diverse climates, living spaces, and cultural practices prevail, selecting the right breed becomes even more significant. From the bustling city streets of Mumbai to the serene countryside of Kerala, there is a perfect pooch for every Indian household. Here, we delve into some of the most suitable dog breeds for pets in India, considering factors such as climate tolerance, living space requirements, and temperament.

1. **Labrador Retriever:** One of the most popular dog breeds worldwide, the Labrador retriever, also shines as an excellent choice for Indian households. Their friendly demeanor, adaptability, and moderate exercise needs make them ideal for urban apartments or spacious rural homes alike. Labs thrive in various climates and are known for their affectionate nature, making them perfect companions for families and individuals alike.
2. **Indian Pariah Dog:** Often overlooked in favor of pedigreed breeds, the Indian Pariah Dog, also known as the Desi Dog, is a resilient and low-maintenance choice for Indian pet owners. These indigenous dogs have evolved to survive in diverse Indian environments, boasting robust health and an innate ability to adapt to local conditions. Indian Pariahs are typically intelligent, loyal, and well-suited to both apartment living and rural settings, making them a favorite among many Indian households.
3. **Pomeranian:** For those seeking a smaller breed with a big personality, the Pomeranian fits the bill perfectly. Their compact size makes them suitable for apartment living, while their lively disposition adds cheer to any home. Pomeranians are well-suited to India's warmer climates and require moderate exercise, making them an excellent choice for individuals or families with limited outdoor space.
4. **Beagle:** Beagles are renowned for their friendly nature and boundless energy, making them a popular choice for active Indian families. Their moderate size and adaptable temperament make them suitable for both urban and rural environments, provided they receive sufficient exercise and mental stimulation. Beagles thrive in the company of humans and other dogs, making them an excellent choice for multi-pet households.
5. **Dachshund:** The Dachshund, with its distinctive long body and short legs, is a beloved breed among Indian pet owners. Their compact size and low exercise needs make them well-suited to apartment living, while

their playful personality adds joy to any home. Dachshunds are relatively low maintenance in terms of grooming and thrive in moderate climates, making them an excellent choice for Indian households seeking a small yet spirited companion.

Conclusion

When choosing a dog breed for a pet in India, it's essential to consider factors such as climate tolerance, living space requirements, and temperament. Whether you reside in a bustling metropolis or a tranquil village, there's a perfect pooch waiting to become a part of your family. By selecting a breed that aligns with your lifestyle and preferences, you can ensure a harmonious and fulfilling relationship with your canine companion for years to come

2

Keep Your Furry Companion Cool and Safe in Summer

As the temperature rises during the summer months, it's crucial for pet owners to be vigilant about the well-being of their furry companions, especially dogs. As dogs are very much playful and active in nature, constant monitoring or observation is required to assess onset of heat stress as its onset is very quick and require immediate attention. Hence, knowing the sign and symptoms of heat stress will save the pets from ensuing negative impact on the health. Proper care and management are essential to ensure your pet stays healthy and happy during this adverse climatic condition.

Dogs release their body temperature through panting and by sweating through the nose and paw pads. If they can't dissipate heat sufficiently their internal body temperature raises leading to hyperthermia (excess body temperature than normal, 101.0 to 102.50F).

Signs and symptoms of heat stress

The signs and symptoms vary as per the degree of stress incurred. At the initial stage of stress they show – ***increased thirst and panting.***

If the situation was not handled then the stress may progress further (heat exhaustion) and the dog will show the symptoms of - ***heavy panting, weak or dullness and episodes of collapsing.***

If treatment was not provided till that stage situation may further progress to **heat stroke** and the symptoms will be –

1. Bright red or pale gum colour
2. Drooling of saliva
3. Dull and dizzy
4. Respiration and heart rate will increase
5. Vomiting and some may show diarrhoea
6. Muscle tremors and seizures

Emergency care during heat stress

If you notice any of the above symptoms then follow the below steps –

1. Take your pet to a cool shaded place or to an air-conditioner room
2. Offer fresh cool water
3. Wet the body (not face), don't put wet towel over the body, it will trap the body heat.
4. Provide fan to evaporate the water and cool the pet
5. Along with this call your consultant Vet for further treatment.

Management during summer to avoid heat stress

1. Hydration is Key

One of the most critical aspects of summer care for dogs is ensuring they stay well-hydrated. Always provide fresh, clean water for your dog, both indoors and outdoors. Consider investing in a pet fountain or multiple water bowls placed strategically throughout your home and yard. Additionally, carry water and a portable bowl when going for walks or outings with your dog to prevent dehydration.

2. Limit Outdoor Activities

During the hottest parts of the day, it's best to limit outdoor activities for your dog. Schedule your walk and playtime during the cooler part of the day when the sun is less intense. Avoid hot pavement or surfaces that can burn your dogs paw pads. Opt for grassy areas or shaded paths for walk.

3. Provide Adequate Shade and Ventilation

If your dog spends time outdoors, ensure there is plenty of shade available. Set up a canopy or place a dog-house in a shaded area where your pet can retreat to escape the sun's rays. Additionally, make sure there is proper ventilation in your home to prevent overheating, especially if you leave your dog indoors during the day.

4. Never Leave Your Dog in a Parked Car

It's a common misconception that cracking the windows of a parked car is sufficient to keep it cool for a dog. The temperature inside a parked car can skyrocket within minutes, even with the windows partially open, leading to heatstroke or even death. Never leave your dog unattended in a parked car, even for a short period, during the summer months.

5. Watch for Signs of Heat Stress

Be vigilant for signs of heat stress in your dog mentioned above. If you suspect your dog is overheating, immediately move them to a cooler environment, offer water, and wet their fur with cool (not cold) water. Seek veterinary attention immediately.

6. Protect Against Parasites

Summer is prime time for parasites like fleas, ticks, and mosquitoes. Protect your dog by using flea and tick preventatives recommended by your veterinarian and keeping up with regular grooming. Additionally, consider using pet-safe mosquito repellents to prevent mosquito-borne diseases like heartworm.

7. Maintain a Healthy Diet

A balanced diet is crucial for your dog's overall health, including their ability to regulate body temperature during the summer. Avoid overfeeding and opt for smaller, more frequent meals to prevent digestive issues. Incorporate fresh fruits and vegetables into their diet for added hydration and nutrients.

Conclusion

Summer can be a fun and enjoyable time for you and your canine companion, but it's essential to prioritize their health and safety during the hot months. By following these tips for care and management, you can ensure your dog stays cool, comfortable, and healthy all summer long.

3

Springtime Care Tips for Your Beloved Canine Companion

As the chill of winter fades away, and nature begins to bloom, it's time to embrace the joys of spring with your furry friend by your side. While spring brings about a sense of renewal and excitement, it also brings some unique challenges for pet owners. Here are some essential tips to ensure your pet dog stays happy, healthy, and safe during the spring season:

1. Regular Grooming Sessions: Springtime means shedding season for many dogs, as they lose their winter coats to make way for lighter ones. Regular grooming sessions, including brushing and bathing, can help reduce shedding and prevent matting. Additionally, grooming helps in checking for any ticks, fleas, or skin irritations that may arise as the weather warms up.
2. Watch Out for Allergies: Just like humans, dogs can suffer from seasonal allergies too. Keep an eye out for signs such as excessive scratching, licking, or sneezing. Consult your veterinarian if you suspect your dog is experiencing allergies, as they can recommend appropriate treatment options or medication.
3. Protect Against Fleas and Ticks: Springtime brings a surge in flea and tick activity. Ensure your dog is up to date on flea and tick prevention medications recommended by your veterinarian. Regularly inspect your pet for any signs of these pests, especially after outdoor activities in grassy or wooded areas.
4. Stay Hydrated: Warmer weather means increased activity levels for both you and your dog. Make sure your pet has access to clean and fresh water at all times, especially during outdoor excursions. Dehydration can be a serious concern, so carry water and a portable bowl when going for walks or hikes.
5. Exercise Caution with Plants and Garden Products: While flowers and plants add beauty to your garden, some can be toxic to dogs if ingested. Research pet-safe options for your garden and keep toxic plants out of

reach. Similarly, be cautious with fertilizers, pesticides, and herbicides, as they can be harmful if ingested or absorbed through the skin.

6. Practice Responsible Walking: Springtime means more outdoor walks and adventures with your dog. Ensure your pet is wearing a collar with proper identification tags and is leashed when in public areas. Be mindful of potential hazards such as puddles, mud, or unfamiliar wildlife during your walks.
7. Maintain a Healthy Diet: With increased activity levels, your dog's nutritional needs may change during the spring season. Consult with your veterinarian to ensure your pet's diet is well-balanced and appropriate for their age, size, and activity level. Avoid feeding your dog table scraps or foods that may be harmful, such as chocolate or grapes.
8. Monitor for Seasonal Ailments: Springtime can exacerbate certain health conditions in dogs, such as hot spots, ear infections, or respiratory issues. Keep an eye out for any signs of discomfort or illness, and seek prompt veterinary care if needed.

By following these springtime care tips, you can ensure your beloved canine companion enjoys the season to the fullest while staying healthy and safe. Remember, a little extra care and attention goes a long way in keeping your pet happy and thriving throughout the year.

4

Winter Care Guide: Keeping Your Furry Friend Safe and Cozy

As the temperature drops and snowflakes begin to fall, it's essential to ensure that your beloved canine companion stays warm, healthy, and happy during the winter months. While winter brings its own set of challenges for pet owners, with some extra care and attention, you can make sure your pet thrives even in the coldest of seasons. Here are some essential tips for caring for and managing your pet dog during winter:

1. Provide Adequate Shelter: If your dog spends time outdoors, make sure they have a warm and dry shelter to retreat to when the weather gets harsh. Whether it's a sturdy doghouse or a cozy insulated shelter, ensure it provides protection from wind, rain, snow, and low temperatures. Consider adding blankets or straw bedding for extra warmth.
2. Limit Outdoor Exposure: While dogs may enjoy playing in the snow, it's crucial to limit their time outdoors during extreme cold weather. Frostbite and hypothermia are real dangers for dogs, especially those with short fur or small breeds. Keep outdoor activities short and supervise your dog closely to prevent any weather-related emergencies.
3. Protect Their Paws: Snow, ice, and road salt can be harsh on your dog's paws, causing irritation, dryness, and even chemical burns. Invest in a pair of dog booties to protect their paws during walks or consider using paw balms to moisturize and create a protective barrier. After walks, wipe your dog's paws with a warm, damp cloth to remove any salt or ice-melting chemicals.
4. Maintain a Healthy Diet: During winter, your dog may burn more calories to stay warm, so it's essential to adjust their diet accordingly. Consult with your veterinarian to determine if your pet needs additional calories or a change in diet to maintain a healthy weight. Adequate hydration is also crucial, so make sure your dog has access to fresh water at all times.
5. Keep Them Groomed: Regular grooming is essential even during winter, as it helps maintain your dog's coat health and hygiene. However, avoid

trimming your dog's fur too short, as longer fur provides added insulation against the cold. Pay extra attention to drying your dog thoroughly after baths to prevent them from getting chilled.

6. Watch Out for Antifreeze: Antifreeze, often used in cars during winter, is highly toxic to dogs if ingested. Keep antifreeze containers securely closed and clean up any spills immediately. Look out for signs of antifreeze poisoning, such as vomiting, diarrhea, lethargy, and seizures, and seek veterinary care immediately if you suspect your dog has been exposed.
7. Stay Active Indoors: On days when outdoor activities are limited, find ways to keep your dog mentally and physically stimulated indoors. Interactive toys, puzzle feeders, and indoor games like fetch or hide-and-seek can help prevent boredom and keep your pet active and engaged.

8. Regular Veterinary Check-ups: Winter weather can exacerbate certain health conditions in dogs, such as arthritis or respiratory issues. Schedule regular veterinary check-ups to monitor your pet's health and address any concerns promptly. Your vet can also provide advice on winter-specific care and recommend any necessary vaccinations or preventive medications.

By following these winter care tips, you can ensure that your pet dog stays safe, healthy, and comfortable throughout the colder months. With a little extra care and attention, you and your furry friend can enjoy the winter wonderland together without any worries.

5

Common Diseases in Pet Dogs and Prevention Measures: A Comprehensive Guide

Ensuring the health and well-being of your pet dog is a top priority for every responsible pet owner. Understanding common diseases that affect dogs and taking preventive measures can significantly improve their quality of life and longevity. Here's an overview of some prevalent canine diseases and how to prevent them:

1. Parvovirus (Parvo)

- Parvovirus is a highly contagious viral disease that affects dogs, especially puppies.
- Symptoms include severe vomiting, diarrhea (often bloody), lethargy, and dehydration.
- Prevention: Vaccination is the most effective way to prevent parvovirus. Puppies should receive a series of vaccinations starting at 6-8 weeks of age, with boosters every few weeks until they are 16-20 weeks old.

2. Canine Distemper

- Canine distemper is a viral disease that affects multiple organ systems, including the respiratory, gastrointestinal, and nervous systems.
- Symptoms include fever, nasal and eye discharge, coughing, vomiting, diarrhea, seizures, and paralysis.
- Prevention: Vaccination is the best way to prevent distemper. Puppies should receive a series of vaccinations, followed by boosters throughout their lives.

3. Rabies

- Rabies is a viral disease that affects the nervous system and is almost always fatal once symptoms appear.

- Symptoms include behavior changes, aggression, paralysis, and eventually death.
- Prevention: Vaccination is crucial for preventing rabies. Many countries and states require dogs to be vaccinated against rabies by law. Keep your dog's rabies vaccination up to date according to local regulations.

4. Heartworm Disease

- Heartworm disease is caused by parasitic worms that are transmitted through mosquito bites and can infect the heart, lungs, and blood vessels of dogs.
- Symptoms include coughing, difficulty breathing, fatigue, and weight loss.
- Prevention: Monthly heartworm preventives are highly effective at protecting dogs against heartworm disease. Consult your veterinarian to determine the best preventive option for your pet.

5. Fleas and Ticks

- Fleas and ticks are external parasites that can cause irritation, itching, and transmit diseases such as Lyme disease and ehrlichiosis.
- Prevention: Use year-round flea and tick preventives recommended by your veterinarian. Regularly check your dog for fleas and ticks, especially after outdoor activities, and promptly remove any parasites found.

6. Obesity

- Obesity is a common health problem in dogs and can lead to various other health issues such as diabetes, joint problems, and heart disease.
- Prevention: Feed your dog a balanced diet appropriate for their age, size, and activity level. Monitor their food intake and avoid overfeeding. Provide regular exercise to help maintain a healthy weight.

7. Dental Disease

- Dental disease is prevalent in dogs and can lead to tooth loss, gum inflammation, and systemic health issues.
- Prevention: Practice good dental hygiene by brushing your dog's teeth regularly, providing dental chews or toys, and scheduling professional dental cleanings as recommended by your veterinarian.

8. Regular Veterinary Care

- Regular veterinary check-ups are essential for maintaining your dog's health & detecting any potential issues early on. Follow your veterinarian's recommendations for vaccinations, parasite prevention, and wellness exams.

By being proactive about preventive healthcare measures and staying vigilant for any signs of illness or discomfort, you can help keep your pet dog happy, healthy, and thriving for years to come. Remember, prevention is always better than cure when it comes to your furry friend's well-being.

6

A Guide to Skin Care and Management for Your Pet Dog

A dog's skin is not only their largest organ but also a vital indicator of their overall health and well-being. Proper skin care and management are essential for keeping your furry friend comfortable, happy, and healthy. Here's a comprehensive guide to maintaining your pet dog's skin:

1. Regular Grooming

- Regular grooming is key to keeping your dog's skin clean and free from debris, dirt, and excess oils. Brushing your dog's coat helps distribute natural oils and prevents matting, which can lead to skin irritation.
- Use a grooming brush appropriate for your dog's coat type and length. Long-haired breeds may require daily brushing, while short-haired breeds may need less frequent grooming.

2. Bathing Routine

- Bathing helps remove dirt, allergens, and bacteria from your dog's skin and coat. However, over-bathing can strip away natural oils and lead to dryness and irritation.
- Use a mild, hypoallergenic dog shampoo specifically formulated for pets. Avoid using human shampoos, as they can be too harsh for your dog's skin.
- Frequency of bathing depends on your dog's breed, lifestyle, and skin condition. Generally, bathing once every 4-6 weeks is sufficient for most dogs.

3. Moisturizing

- Just like humans, dogs can experience dry skin, especially in dry or cold climates. Moisturizing can help soothe dry, itchy skin and prevent flakiness.

- Choose a pet-safe moisturizer or skin conditioner and apply it sparingly to your dog's skin, focusing on areas prone to dryness such as elbows, hocks, and paw pads.
- Consult your veterinarian before using any topical products on your dog's skin, especially if they have pre-existing skin conditions or allergies.

4. Nutrition and Hydration

- A balanced diet rich in essential nutrients is crucial for maintaining your dog's skin health from the inside out. Omega-3 fatty acids, vitamins, and minerals play a key role in promoting healthy skin and a shiny coat.
- Ensure your dog has access to clean, fresh water at all times to stay hydrated. Proper hydration is essential for maintaining skin elasticity and preventing dryness.

5. Flea and Tick Control

- Fleas and ticks not only cause discomfort and irritation but can also transmit diseases and lead to skin infections.
- Use veterinarian-recommended flea and tick preventives year-round to protect your dog from infestations. Regularly check your dog for signs of fleas and ticks, especially after outdoor activities.

6. Allergy Management

- Dogs can suffer from allergies to various environmental triggers, including pollen, dust, mold, and certain foods. Allergic reactions often manifest as itching, redness, and skin irritation.
- Work with your veterinarian to identify and manage your dog's allergies. This may involve allergy testing, dietary changes, medications, or immunotherapy (allergy shots).

7. Sun Protection

- Dogs with light-colored or thin coats are susceptible to sunburn and skin damage from prolonged sun exposure. Protect your dog's skin by limiting outdoor activities during peak sun hours and providing shade when outdoors.
- Consider using pet-safe sunscreen on exposed areas such as the nose, ears, and belly, especially for dogs with short or thin fur.

8. Regular Veterinary Check-ups

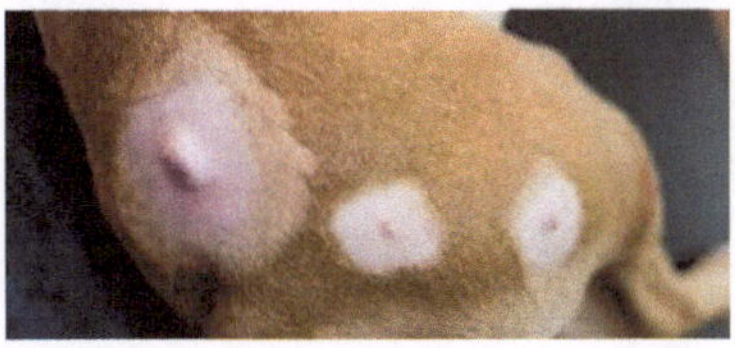

- Schedule regular veterinary exams to monitor your dog's skin health and address any concerns promptly. Your veterinarian can provide personalized recommendations for skin care based on your dog's breed, age, & individual needs.

By incorporating these skin care and management practices into your pet care routine, you can help keep your dog's skin healthy, comfortable, and radiant. Remember to be observant of any changes in your dog's skin condition and seek veterinary advice if you notice persistent irritation, itching, or other abnormalities. With proper care, your furry friend can enjoy healthy skin and a happy, itch-free life.

7

Essential Eye and Ear Care: Maintaining Your Pet Dog's Sensory Health

The eyes and ears are not only vital sensory organs for your pet dog but also key indicators of their overall health and well-being. Proper care and management of these delicate areas are essential for preventing infections, maintaining comfort, and preserving your furry friend's quality of life. Here's a comprehensive guide to eye and ear care for pet dogs:

Eye Care

1. Regular Inspection

- Start by regularly inspecting your dog's eyes for any signs of redness, swelling, discharge, or cloudiness. Clear, bright eyes indicate good health, while any changes may signal an underlying issue.
- Look out for excessive tearing, squinting, or rubbing of the eyes, as these may indicate irritation or injury.

2. Gentle Cleaning

- Use a clean, damp cloth or sterile saline solution to gently wipe away any debris or discharge from around your dog's eyes. Be careful not to touch the eyeball itself.
- If your dog has tear stains, use a specially formulated tear stain remover recommended by your veterinarian to safely clean the area around the eyes.

3. Preventing Irritants

- Keep your dog's hair around the eyes trimmed to prevent it from irritating the eyes or causing tear stains.
- Avoid using harsh chemicals or products near your dog's eyes, including household cleaners, shampoos, and insect repellents.

4. Protecting Against UV Damage

- Dogs with light-colored or thin fur around their eyes are susceptible to sunburn and UV damage. Consider using pet-safe sunscreen or providing your dog with UV-protective sunglasses when outdoors for extended periods.

5. Regular Veterinary Exams

- Schedule regular veterinary check-ups to monitor your dog's eye health and detect any potential issues early on. Your veterinarian can perform a comprehensive eye exam and provide recommendations for preventive care and treatment if needed.

By incorporating these eye and ear care practices into your pet care routine, you can help ensure that your dog's sensory health remains in optimal condition. Remember to be observant of any changes in your dog's eyes or ears and seek veterinary advice if you notice persistent issues or abnormalities. With proper care and attention, you can keep your furry friend's eyes bright and ears healthy for years to come.

8

Understanding Normal Behavior in Pet Dogs: A Guide for Pet Owners

As cherished members of our families, pet dogs bring joy, companionship, and unconditional love into our lives. Understanding their normal behavior is essential for building a strong bond and providing the care and support they need to thrive. Here's a comprehensive guide to the typical behavior of pet dogs:

1. Social Behavior

- Dogs are social animals and thrive on companionship and interaction with humans and other animals. They often seek out attention, affection, and physical contact from their owners.
- Common social behaviors include wagging their tails, licking, leaning against their owners, and seeking proximity during rest or sleep.

2. Playfulness

- Playfulness is a natural behavior in dogs and serves multiple purposes, including physical exercise, mental stimulation, and social bonding.
- Dogs may engage in various play behaviors such as chasing, fetching, tug-of-war, and interactive games with their owners or other dogs.

3. Communication

- Dogs communicate through a combination of vocalizations, body language, and facial expressions. Understanding their communication cues is essential for interpreting their needs and emotions.
- Common communication signals include barking, growling, whining, ear position, tail wagging, and facial expressions such as relaxed or tense muscles.

4. Exploratory Behavior

- Dogs are naturally curious creatures and enjoy exploring their environment through sniffing, digging, and investigating new sights, sounds, and smells.

- Providing opportunities for exploration, such as outdoor walks, interactive toys, and enrichment activities, helps satisfy their natural instincts and mental stimulation needs.

5. Territorial Behavior

- Dogs may exhibit territorial behavior to establish and defend their territory, which can include their home, yard, or favorite resting spots.
- Signs of territorial behavior may include barking at perceived intruders, marking with urine or scent glands, and displaying protective body language.

6. Sleep Patterns

- Dogs typically spend a significant portion of their day sleeping, ranging from 12 to 14 hours for adult dogs and even more for puppies and senior dogs.
- Dogs may exhibit different sleep patterns, including short naps throughout the day and longer periods of deep sleep during the night.

7. Eating Habits

- Dogs have individual eating habits and preferences, but most exhibit healthy appetites and enjoy mealtime.
- Common eating behaviors include eagerly approaching their food bowl, wagging their tails while eating, chewing food thoroughly, and occasionally burying or hiding food items.

8. Grooming Behavior

- Dogs engage in grooming behaviors to maintain their hygiene and appearance. This includes licking themselves to clean their fur, scratching to remove loose hair and debris, and occasionally rolling in dirt or grass.
- Some dogs may also exhibit grooming behaviors towards their owners or other dogs as a form of social bonding and affection.

9. Anxiety and Stress

- While dogs are generally resilient and adaptable, they may experience anxiety or stress in response to certain situations, such as loud noises, unfamiliar environments, or changes in routine.
- Signs of anxiety or stress may include panting, pacing, trembling, hiding, excessive drooling, and destructive behavior.

Understanding and appreciating your dog's normal behavior is the foundation for building a strong, trusting relationship. By providing love, companionship, proper care, and enrichment, you can ensure that your pet dog lives a happy, fulfilling life as a cherished member of your family.

9

Exercise Guide for Dogs

In today's sedentary lifestyle, ensuring adequate exercise for pet dogs is crucial for their physical health, mental well-being and preventing obesity. To help pet owners understand the importance of exercise in maintaining the overall health and happiness their canine companions and how much exercise is adequate to different pet breeds are incorporated in this text.

Physical Health Benefits

Regular physical activity is essential for controlling weight and preventing obesity, which are common concerns among dogs. Obesity in dogs is associated with various health issues such as diabetes, heart disease, and arthritis. Engaging in activities like walking, running, and playing not only burns calories but also improves cardiovascular health, strengthens muscles, and enhances flexibility.

Mental Well-being

Exercise plays a crucial role in stimulating mental health and reducing behavioral problems in dogs. Adequate physical activity helps in alleviating boredom, anxiety, and destructive or aggressive behaviors in dogs. Dogs that receive regular exercise exhibit reduced levels of stress and exhibit improved cognitive function compared to sedentary counterparts.

Socialization and Bonding

Exercise provides valuable opportunities for socialization and bonding between pet dogs and their owners. Activities such as group walks, visits to the dog park, or obedience training classes not only promote physical health but also nurture social bonds, leading to a more fulfilling relationship between pets and their owners.

Various types of exercise for dog

1. **Walking**
2. **Jogging / cycling**
3. **Swimming:** make sure the area is safe i.e no strong current, deep water etc.

4. **Agility sports:** it is a sport where the dog-handler guides the dog around an obstacle course
5. **Flyball:** good for high activity levels dog
6. **Play dates:** join with other dog lovers
7. **Brain games:** teaching new tricks, food puzzles, toys etc.

Routine Exercise Recommendations

To ensure optimal health and well-being, pet owners should tailor the exercise regimen as per their dog's breed, age, and individual needs. Here are few specific exercise recommendations for different types of dog breeds:

1. High-Energy Breeds (e.g., Border Collies, Australian Shepherds)

- Daily vigorous exercise such as running, hiking, or playing fetch for at least 60-90 minutes.
- Engage in mentally stimulating activities like agility or flyball to challenge their intelligence and energy.

2. Medium-Energy Breeds (e.g., Labrador Retrievers, Golden Retrievers)

- Daily brisk walks or jogs for 30-60 minutes.
- Interactive play sessions with toys like balls or frisbees to keep them physically and mentally engaged.

3. Low-Energy Breeds (e.g., Bulldogs, Basset Hounds)

- Short walks multiple times a day, totaling 30-45 minutes.
- Gentle activities like indoor play or scent games to prevent obesity and boredom.

4. Brachycephalic Breeds (e.g., Pugs, Bulldogs)

- Avoid strenuous exercise in hot or humid weather due to their respiratory issues.
- Short, leisurely walks and indoor playtime to prevent overexertion.

5. Toy Breeds (e.g., Chihuahuas, Toy Poodles)

- Short walks or indoor play sessions tailored to their size and energy levels.
- Mental stimulation through obedience training or puzzle toys to keep their minds sharp.

Exercise in obese dogs

1. Introduce exercise slow and gradually, one can start by 10 minutes session in morning and evening
2. Gradually increase the time, this will vary dog to dog, hence, careful assessment is required.
3. Frequently change the walking route; it will be fun for the dog.
4. Add fun games e.g. balls, friebees etc.
5. Keep proper vigil during the introduction of exercise; never force the dog if you notice exhaustion or any behavioural changes.

Precautions or injuries during exercise

1. Avoid high-activity exercise in brachycephalic (flat faces and short nose) breeds of dog especially in summer.
2. Avoid throwing sticks as a fetch, as it may cause choking
3. Avoid walking or jogging in hot pavements it may injure the paw pads.
4. Muscle, joint or ligaments injuries may occur during high-activity exercise. Immediately consult with your Vet.

5. Heat stroke- if exercise is done in very sunny days esp. in brachycephalic breeds, obese dogs etc.

By incorporating breed-specific exercises into their daily routine, pet owners can ensure that their furry friends receive the appropriate amount of physical activity and mental stimulation to lead happy and healthy lives.

Conclusion

Prioritizing regular exercise for pet dogs is essential for their overall health and well-being. Whether it's daily walks, interactive playtime, or participating in breed-specific activities, providing opportunities for physical activity and mental stimulation is key to ensuring a fulfilling life for our canine companions.

10

Oral Care for Pet Dogs An In-Depth Guide

Maintaining your dog's oral hygiene is crucial for their overall health and happiness. Dental issues can lead to pain, infection and even systemic health problems affecting vital organs. This comprehensive guide delves deeper into the importance of oral care, step-by-step techniques for cleaning your dog's teeth, signs of dental issues and tips for maintaining optimal oral health.

Importance of Oral Care

1. Preventing Periodontal Disease

Stages of Periodontal Disease: This common dental issue progresses through stages, starting with gingivitis (inflammation of the gums) and advancing to periodontitis, where the supporting structures of the teeth are damaged. Untreated periodontal disease can lead to tooth loss and infections that can spread to different tissues including gastrointestinal tract, liver, heart and kidneys.

2. Avoiding Bad Breath (Halitosis)

Causes: Bad breath is primarily caused by microbial buildup in the mouth due to poor oral hygiene. Persistent bad breath can be a sign of more serious dental problems.

3. Improving Overall Health

Systemic Health: Dental infections can enter the bloodstream, leading to systemic health issues including endocarditis (infection of the heart valves) and sepsis. Maintaining good oral health improves your dog's quality of life, reducing pain and discomfort.

Techniques for Cleaning Your Dog's Teeth

1. Brushing Your Dog's Teeth

Choosing the Right Tools: Use a dog-specific toothbrush or a finger brush. Dog toothpaste is formulated to be safe for dogs if swallowed and often comes in flavors they enjoy, like poultry or peanut butter.

Introducing Brushing

- Start by allowing your dog taste the toothpaste.
- Gradually introduce the brush by gently lifting their lips and brushing a few teeth at a time.
- Be patient and make the experience positive with praise and treats.

Brushing Technique

- Hold the brush at a 45-degree angle to the teeth.
- Use small circular motions, focusing on the gum line.
- Brush both the outside and inside surfaces of the teeth.
- Aim to brush for about two minutes, but start with shorter sessions to build your dog's tolerance.

2. Dental Chews and Toys

These products can help reduce plaque and tartar buildup through mechanical action as your dog chews. Look for products approved by the Veterinary Oral Health Council (VOHC), which certifies the effectiveness of dental health products for pets.

3. Water Additives

These additives are mixed with your dog's drinking water and can help reduce plaque and freshen breath. Consult your veterinarian to choose a safe and effective product.

4. Diet and Nutrition

A balanced diet supports overall health including dental health. However, apart from providing a balanced diet some dog foods are specifically formulated to reduce plaque and tartar buildup on teeth.

Signs and symptoms of Dental Issues

1. Bad Breath: While some dog breath is normal, persistent bad breath is often a sign of dental disease.
2. Inflamed or Bleeding Gums: Red, swollen, or bleeding gums can indicate gingivitis or periodontal disease.
3. Tartar Buildup: Yellow or brown tartar on the teeth is a sign of plaque accumulation and poor oral hygiene.
4. Difficulty Eating: Reluctance to eat, dropping food, or chewing on one side of the mouth can indicate dental problems.

5. Loose or Missing Teeth: Loose teeth or noticeable tooth loss requires immediate veterinary attention.
6. Behavioral Changes: Changes in behavior, such as irritability or withdrawal can be signs of dental discomfort.

Tips for Maintaining Optimal Oral Health

1. Regular Dental Check-Ups

Schedule a regular dental check-up with your veterinarian at least once in a year. Your vet can provide guidance on the best oral care practices and products for your dog.

2. Professional Cleanings

Professional cleanings are performed to a pet under medications (anesthesia) to thoroughly clean the teeth and address any issues that brushing alone cannot solve. The frequency of professional cleanings depends on your dog's oral health and your veterinarian's recommendations.

3. Daily Brushing

Consistency is the key to prevent plaque and tartar buildup. Aim to brush your dog's teeth daily. Make brushing a part of your dog's daily routine to increase their comfort with the process.

4. Monitor Oral Health

Regularly check your dog's mouth for signs of dental issues. Lift their lips to examine their gums and teeth. Early detection of dental problems can prevent more serious health issues.

5. Healthy Chews

Provide safe, vet-approved chew toys and treats that promote dental health. Chews should be appropriately sized for your dog to prevent choking and ensure they are effective in reducing plaque.

Conclusion

Oral care is a vital component of your dog's overall health regimen. By incorporating regular brushing, providing dental-friendly treats and toys, scheduling routine veterinary check-ups, you can ensure your dog's teeth and gums stay healthy. Maintaining your dog's oral hygiene will not only improve their quality of life but also prevent serious health issues down the road. With proper care, you can keep your furry friend's smile bright and their breath fresh for years to come.

11

Care and Management of Dogs During Travel: A Comprehensive Guide

Traveling with your dog can be a delightful experience, whether you're embarking on a road trip, flying to a distant destination, or simply visiting friends and family. However, it requires careful planning and preparation to ensure your dog's safety, comfort, and well-being. This guide covers the essential aspects of traveling with your dog, providing tips and best practices for a smooth journey.

Preparing for the Journey

Health Check and Documentation

1. Veterinary Check-up: Before any trip, schedule a visit to the vet to ensure your dog is healthy and up-to-date on vaccinations. Discuss any travel-specific health concerns with your vet.
2. Documentation: Carry a copy of your dog’s medical records, including vaccination certificates, in case they are needed during your trip. Some destinations require proof of rabies vaccination and other health certifications.

Travel Essentials

1. Identification: Ensure your dog wears a collar with an ID tag containing your contact information. A microchip is an additional safety measure.
2. Comfort Items: Bring your dog’s favorite toys, bedding, and a familiar blanket to help reduce stress and provide comfort.
3. Travel Kit: Pack a travel kit with food, water, bowls, medications, a leash, waste bags, grooming supplies, and a first-aid kit.

Traveling by Car

Safety First

1. Restraints: Use a dog seat belt, harness, or crate to secure your dog in the car. This prevents distractions while driving and protects your dog in case of sudden stops or accidents.

2. Temperature Control: Never leave your dog alone in a parked car, especially in hot or cold weather. Temperatures can quickly become dangerous.

Comfort and Well-being

1. Regular Breaks: Stop every 2-3 hours to allow your dog to stretch, relieve themselves, and drink water. Exercise helps reduce anxiety and restlessness.
2. Hydration and Feeding: Keep water available for your dog, especially on long trips. Feed them a light meal a few hours before travel to prevent motion sickness. Avoid feeding your dog during the journey to reduce the risk of nausea.

Minimizing Anxiety

1. Calm Environment: Maintain a calm and quiet environment in the car. Playing soft music or using a calming spray can help reduce anxiety.
2. Desensitization: Gradually acclimate your dog to car travel by taking short trips and gradually increasing the duration.

Traveling by Air

Pre-Flight Preparation

1. Airline Policies: Check the airline's pet travel policies, including crate requirements, documentation, and any restrictions on breed or size.
2. Health Certificate: Obtain a health certificate from your vet within the timeframe required by the airline, usually within 10 days of travel.

Choosing the Right Crate

1. Size and Comfort: Select a well-ventilated, airline-approved crate that allows your dog to stand, turn around, and lie down comfortably. Line the crate with an absorbent pad and a familiar blanket.
2. Identification: Label the crate with your contact information, your destination, and a "Live Animal" sticker.

During the Flight

1. Pre-Flight Exercise: Ensure your dog gets plenty of exercise before the flight to help them relax.
2. In-Flight Care: If your dog is traveling in the cabin, keep them calm and reassured. For dogs in the cargo hold, ensure they have a secure and comfortable setup.

Traveling by Train or Bus

Pet Policies: Check the pet policies of the train or bus company. Some may have restrictions on size or breed, or may require pets to be in carriers.

Comfort and Safety

1. Carrier Use: Use a sturdy, well-ventilated carrier for your dog. Ensure they have enough space to move comfortably.
2. Frequent Breaks: Plan for regular breaks to allow your dog to relieve themselves and stretch, especially on long trips.

Accommodations

Pet-Friendly Lodging: pet-friendly hotels, motels, or vacation rentals in advance. Confirm their pet policies and any additional fees.

1. In-Room Comfort: Create a comfortable space in your room with your dog's bedding and toys. Ensure they have access to fresh water.

Maintaining Routine

1. Familiar Environment: Try to maintain your dog's routine as much as possible. Regular feeding times, walks, and playtime help reduce stress.
2. Exercise: Find nearby parks or walking trails where your dog can get regular exercise.

General Tips for a Smooth Journey

Behavior and Training

- Basic Commands: Ensure your dog responds well to basic commands like sit, stay, and come. Good behavior is essential in unfamiliar environments.
- Socialization: Expose your dog to different environments and situations before your trip to help them adapt more easily.

Emergency Preparedness

- Local Vet Information: note down the contact information of veterinarians near your travel destination.
- First-Aid Kit: Include bandages, antiseptic wipes, tweezers, and any medications your dog may need.

Minimizing Stress

- Comfort Items: Bring items that smell like home to comfort your dog.
- Patience and Reassurance: Stay calm and patient with your dog, offering reassurance and attention to keep them calm.

Conclusion

Traveling with your dog can be a wonderful experience with the right preparation and care. By planning ahead, ensuring safety, and providing comfort, you can make the journey enjoyable for both you and your canine companion. Whether you're traveling by car, air, train, or bus, these tips will help ensure a smooth and stress-free trip, allowing you to create lasting memories with your furry friend.

12

Caring for Senior Dogs Health and Comfort

As dogs age, their needs change significantly, requiring adjustments in their care routine to ensure they remain healthy, comfortable, and happy in their golden years. Caring for a senior dog involves paying attention to their evolving physical and emotional needs, managing health issues proactively, and providing a supportive and nurturing environment. This article outlines the key aspects of caring for senior dogs, focusing on health and comfort.

Recognizing When Your Dog is a Senior

Dogs are generally considered seniors at around seven years old, although this can vary depending on breed and size. Larger breeds tend to age faster than smaller breeds. Signs of aging include graying fur, decreased energy levels, stiffness, and changes in behavior or appetite.

Health Care for Senior Dogs

Regular Veterinary Check-ups

Frequency: Increase the frequency of veterinary visits to at least twice a year. Regular check-ups can help detect and manage health issues early.

Comprehensive Exams: Ensure the vet conducts comprehensive exams, including blood tests, dental check-ups, and screenings for common age-related conditions such as arthritis, diabetes, kidney disease, and cancer.

Diet and Nutrition

- Specialized Diet: Switch to a senior dog food formula, which is typically lower in calories but higher in fiber and contains nutrients that support joint health and cognitive function.
- Weight Management: Monitor your dog's weight closely. Obesity can exacerbate health issues, so maintain a balanced diet and avoid overfeeding.
- Supplements: Consider supplements such as glucosamine and chondroitin for joint health, omega-3 fatty acids for skin and coat health, and antioxidants to support the immune system.

Exercise and Mobility

- Gentle Exercise: Regular, low-impact exercise is crucial for maintaining muscle mass and joint flexibility. Short, frequent walks and gentle play sessions are ideal.
- Mobility Aids: Provide mobility aids like ramps, orthopedic beds, and non-slip mats to help your dog move around comfortably and prevent falls.

Dental Care

- Regular Cleaning: Dental health is often overlooked in senior dogs, but it's vital for overall health. Brush your dog's teeth regularly and schedule professional cleanings as needed.
- Monitor for Issues: Watch for signs of dental problems such as bad breath, difficulty eating, or pawing at the mouth, and seek veterinary care promptly.

Comfort and Well-being

Comfortable Living Environment

- Cozy Bedding: Provide a soft, supportive bed to alleviate pressure on joints and ensure your dog has a warm and comfortable place to rest.
- Climate Control: Senior dogs are more sensitive to temperature extremes. Keep your home at a comfortable temperature and provide warm blankets in winter and cooling mats in summer.

Mental Stimulation

- Interactive Toys: Use interactive toys and puzzles to keep your dog's mind active and engaged. Mental stimulation can help slow cognitive decline.
- Training and Socialization: Continue gentle training and socialization activities. Familiar routines and positive interactions help maintain mental sharpness and reduce anxiety.

Routine and Stability

- Consistent Routine: Maintain a consistent daily routine for feeding, exercise, and sleep. Stability helps reduce stress and anxiety in senior dogs.
- Reduced Stress: Minimize changes in the environment and routine to keep your dog comfortable. Avoid loud noises and chaotic environments.

Managing Age-Related Health Issues

Arthritis and Joint Pain

- Medication: Consult your vet about pain management options, including anti-inflammatory medications and joint supplements.
- Physical Therapy: Consider physical therapy or hydrotherapy to improve mobility and reduce pain.

Vision and Hearing Loss

- Adaptations: Make adaptations to your home to help your dog navigate more easily. Keep pathways clear and use tactile cues like textured mats.
- Communication: Learn new ways to communicate with your dog, such as using hand signals or vibrations.

Cognitive Decline

- Veterinary Support: Discuss with your vet any signs of cognitive decline, such as disorientation or changes in behavior, and explore treatment options.
- Enrichment Activities: Engage your dog in enrichment activities that challenge their mind and senses.

Emotional Support and Bonding

Quality Time

- Companionship: Spend quality time with your dog through gentle play, grooming, and simply sitting together. Your presence and attention are incredibly comforting.
- Affection: Show affection through gentle petting and positive reinforcement. Senior dogs still thrive on love and attention.

Monitoring and Responding to Needs

- Observation: Pay close attention to any changes in your dog's behavior, appetite, or mobility. Promptly address any concerns with your veterinarian.
- Adaptability: Be adaptable and patient as your dog's needs change. Providing a loving and supportive environment is key to their well-being.

Conclusion

Caring for a senior dog requires a blend of proactive health management, environmental adaptations, and emotional support. By recognizing the unique needs of older dogs and addressing them with compassion and diligence, you can ensure that your furry companion enjoys a comfortable, happy, and fulfilling life in their golden years. Your commitment to their health and comfort will strengthen the bond you share and create cherished memories together.

13

Care Management of Dogs During Pregnancy and Whelping

Managing the care of a pregnant dog and supporting her through the whelping process requires careful attention, preparation, and understanding. Ensuring the health and safety of both the mother and her puppies is paramount. This article provides a comprehensive guide on how to care for a dog during pregnancy and whelping, including nutritional needs, veterinary care, creating a whelping area, and post-birth care.

Understanding Canine Pregnancy

Gestation Period

- The gestation period for dogs is approximately 63 days, though it can range from 58 to 68 days.

Signs of Pregnancy

- Early signs include increased appetite, slight weight gain, and changes in behavior such as increased affection.
- Around the fourth week, the abdomen may start to swell, and by the sixth week, noticeable weight gain and enlarged nipples are common.

Prenatal Care

Veterinary Visits

- Initial Check-up: Schedule a veterinary appointment as soon as you suspect pregnancy. The vet can confirm pregnancy through palpation, ultrasound, or X-rays and provide guidance on care.
- Regular Monitoring: Regular check-ups throughout the pregnancy are crucial to monitor the health of the mother and the developing puppies.

Nutrition

- Balanced Diet: Feed a high-quality, balanced diet appropriate for pregnant dogs. Consult your vet for specific dietary recommendations.

- Increased Caloric Intake: As pregnancy progresses, increase the mother's caloric intake by 30-50%, especially during the last few weeks.
- Supplements: Your vet may recommend supplements such as folic acid or omega-3 fatty acids to support fetal development.

Exercise

- Moderate Exercise: Maintain regular, moderate exercise to keep the mother healthy and fit. Avoid strenuous activities, especially as the pregnancy advances.
- Gentle Walks: Gentle walks and light play are beneficial. Monitor her closely for signs of fatigue.

Environment

- Comfortable Space: Provide a comfortable, quiet, and safe space for the pregnant dog to rest. Reduce stress and avoid any significant changes to her environment.
- Whelping Area: Prepare a whelping area well in advance. This should be a quiet, warm, and clean space where she feels secure. A whelping box lined with clean towels or blankets works well.

Preparing for Whelping

Whelping Supplies

- Whelping Box: A sturdy, clean whelping box that the mother can easily enter and exit.
- Clean Towels and Blankets: For lining the whelping box and cleaning the puppies.
- Thermometer: To monitor the mother's temperature as whelping approaches (a drop to around 98-99°F indicates labor will start soon).
- Gloves and Lubricant: For assisting with the delivery if necessary.
- Bulb Syringe: To clear the puppies' airways if needed.
- Scale: To weigh the puppies after birth.

Signs of Impending Labor

- Nesting Behavior: The mother may start nesting, digging, or arranging her bedding.
- Temperature Drop: A drop in rectal temperature to around 98-99°F indicates labor is imminent.
- Restlessness and Panting: Increased restlessness, panting, and seeking seclusion are common signs of early labor.

During Whelping

Stages of Labor

1. First Stage: Uterine contractions begin. The mother may appear restless, pant, and refuse food. This stage can last 6-12 hours.
2. Second Stage: Active labor with the delivery of puppies. Each puppy is usually born within 30 minutes to an hour of the previous one. Total whelping time can vary from a few hours to 24 hours.
3. Third Stage: Delivery of the placenta. This occurs after each puppy or sometimes after multiple puppies.

Assisting During Whelping

- Quiet Presence: Stay calm and quiet, offering reassurance but intervening minimally unless necessary.
- Puppy Care: If the mother does not clean a puppy, gently rub the puppy with a clean towel to stimulate breathing. Use a bulb syringe to clear the airway if needed.
- Monitoring: Monitor the mother and puppies closely, ensuring each puppy nurses and is warm.

Post-Whelping Care

Mother's Care

- Nutrition: Continue feeding a high-quality, nutrient-rich diet. Lactating mothers have increased nutritional needs.
- Hydration: Ensure she has constant access to fresh water.
- Rest and Recovery: Allow the mother to rest and recover. Keep the environment calm and stress-free.

Puppy Care

- Warmth: Keep the puppies warm as they cannot regulate their body temperature. Use a heating pad set on low, ensuring there is a cooler area for the mother.
- Nursing: Ensure all puppies are nursing well. Consult your vet if any puppies struggle to latch or seem weak.
- Veterinary Check: Schedule a vet check for the mother and puppies within the first 48 hours after birth.

Monitoring Health

- Signs of Trouble: Watch for signs of trouble such as excessive bleeding, foul-smelling discharge, lethargy, or refusal to nurse in the mother, and failure to gain weight or weakness in the puppies.
- Emergency Care: Contact your vet immediately if you notice any concerning symptoms in the mother or puppies.

Conclusion

Caring for a pregnant dog and supporting her through the whelping process is a rewarding experience that requires attention to detail, preparation, and a lot of love. By providing proper prenatal care, preparing for whelping, and ensuring both the mother and puppies receive appropriate post-birth care, you can help ensure a safe and healthy start for the new family. Always consult your veterinarian for guidance and support throughout the pregnancy and whelping process.

14

Grooming and Hygiene of Pet Dogs

Proper grooming and hygiene are essential for maintaining the health and well-being of pet dogs. Regular grooming not only keeps your dog looking and smelling good but also helps prevent various health issues such as skin infections, parasites, and dental problems. This article explores the key aspects of grooming and hygiene for pet dogs, including brushing, bathing, nail care, ear and eye care, dental hygiene, and general tips for maintaining a clean and healthy canine companion.

Brushing

Benefits

- Reduces Shedding: Regular brushing helps remove loose hair, reducing shedding and keeping your home cleaner.
- Prevents Matting: For dogs with longer coats, brushing prevents mats and tangles, which can cause discomfort and lead to skin issues.
- Stimulates Skin: Brushing stimulates the skin and distributes natural oils, promoting a healthy coat.

Frequency

- Short-Haired Breeds: Brush once a week.
- Long-Haired Breeds: Brush several times a week, or even daily during shedding season.

Tools

- Slicker Brush: Effective for removing tangles and mats.
- Bristle Brush: Suitable for short-haired dogs to remove loose hair and dirt.
- Deshedding Tool: Helps manage shedding for both short and long-haired breeds.

Bathing

Benefits

- Cleanses the Skin and Coat: Removes dirt, debris, and allergens.
- Controls Odor: Keeps your dog smelling fresh.
- Prevents Skin Issues: Helps manage and prevent skin conditions such as dermatitis and fungal infections.

Frequency

- General Recommendation: Bathe your dog once a month.
- Activity Level and Coat Type: Dogs that spend a lot of time outdoors or have oily coats may need more frequent baths, while others may require less frequent bathing.

Steps

1. Brush Before Bathing: Remove tangles and loose hair.
2. Use Lukewarm Water: Ensure the water is not too hot or too cold.
3. Dog-Specific Shampoo: Use a shampoo formulated for dogs to avoid skin irritation.
4. Thorough Rinse: Rinse thoroughly to remove all shampoo residue.
5. Drying: Towel dry or use a dog-safe blow dryer on a low setting.

Nail Care

Importance

- Prevents Pain and Injury: Overgrown nails can cause discomfort and lead to injuries.
- Maintains Proper Posture: Properly trimmed nails prevent gait abnormalities.

Frequency

- Every 3-4 Weeks: Depending on how fast your dog's nails grow.

Steps

1. Use Proper Tools: Use dog nail clippers or a nail grinder.
2. Know the Quick: Be cautious of the quick, the sensitive part of the nail. Trim small amounts to avoid cutting it.
3. Reward and Comfort: Offer treats and praise to keep your dog calm.

Ear and Eye Care

Ear Care

- Check Weekly: Inspect ears for dirt, redness, or odor.
- Cleaning: Use a vet-approved ear cleaner and cotton balls. Avoid inserting anything into the ear canal.

Eye Care

- Check Daily: Look for discharge, redness, or cloudiness.
- Cleaning: Use a damp cloth to gently wipe around the eyes. For breeds prone to tear staining, use a tear stain remover.

Dental Hygiene

Importance

- Prevents Dental Disease: Regular brushing prevents plaque buildup and gum disease.
- Fresh Breath: Reduces bad breath.

Methods

- Brushing: Brush your dog's teeth 2-3 times a week using a dog-specific toothbrush and toothpaste.
- Dental Chews: Provide dental chews that help reduce plaque and tartar.
- Regular Vet Checks: Schedule regular dental check-ups with your vet.

General Hygiene Tips

Anal Gland Care

- Expression: Some dogs may need their anal glands expressed regularly to prevent impaction and infection. Consult your vet or a professional groomer for assistance.

Paw Car

- Inspection: Check paws regularly for cuts, foreign objects, and signs of infection.
- Moisturizing: Use paw balm to keep paw pads soft and prevent cracking.

Maintaining a Clean Environment

- Bedding: Wash your dog's bedding regularly to keep it clean and free of allergens.
- Living Area: Keep your dog's living area clean by vacuuming and disinfecting regularly.

Conclusion

Grooming and hygiene are critical components of responsible pet ownership. Regular grooming sessions provide an opportunity to check your dog for signs of health problems, such as skin issues, ear infections, or dental disease, allowing for early intervention. By establishing a consistent grooming routine, you can ensure that your dog remains healthy, comfortable, and happy, strengthening the bond you share with your furry friend.

15

Reduce the Risk to Pet-Associated Zoonotic Infections

Pets provide companionship, emotional support, and numerous health benefits to their owners. However, they can also be carriers of zoonotic diseases—diseases that can be transmitted from animals to humans. Understanding these risks and implementing measures to reduce them is crucial for maintaining the health and safety of both pets and humans. This article explores common pet-associated zoonotic infections and offers strategies to minimize the risk of transmission.

Common Pet-Associated Zoonotic Infections

1. Rabies

- Cause: Rabies is caused by the rabies virus and is transmitted through the bite of an infected animal.
- Symptoms in Humans: Initial symptoms include fever and headache, progressing to neurological symptoms such as confusion, hallucinations, and paralysis. Rabies is almost always fatal once symptoms appear.
- Prevention: Vaccination of pets, avoiding contact with wild animals, and immediate medical attention after potential exposure.

2. Toxoplasmosis

- Cause: Toxoplasmosis is caused by the parasite Toxoplasma gondii, often found in cat feces.
- Symptoms in Humans: In healthy individuals, symptoms are usually mild and flu-like. In pregnant women and immunocompromised individuals, it can cause severe complications such as birth defects or neurological damage.
- Prevention: Regularly clean cat litter boxes, wash hands thoroughly after handling cat feces, and avoid undercooked meat.

3. Cat Scratch Disease (CSD)

- Cause: CSD is caused by the bacterium Bartonella henselae, transmitted through scratches or bites from infected cats.
- Symptoms in Humans: Symptoms include fever, swollen lymph nodes, and fatigue. Severe cases can affect the eyes, brain, and heart.
- Prevention: Avoid rough play with cats, clean scratches and bites promptly, and control fleas to reduce infection risk in cats.

4. Ringworm

- Cause: Ringworm is a fungal infection that affects the skin, hair, and nails of both animals and humans.
- Symptoms in Humans: It appears as a red, circular, itchy rash. It is highly contagious and can spread through direct contact or contaminated objects.
- Prevention: Maintain good hygiene, regularly clean pet bedding and living areas, and avoid sharing personal items like towels with infected pets.

5. Salmonellosis

- Cause: Salmonellosis is caused by Salmonella bacteria, which can be found in the feces of infected animals, including reptiles, birds, and some mammals.
- Symptoms in Humans: Symptoms include diarrhea, fever, and abdominal cramps. Severe cases can lead to dehydration and hospitalization.
- Prevention: Wash hands thoroughly after handling pets or cleaning up after them, and avoid consuming raw or undercooked eggs and meat.

6. Leptospirosis

- Cause: Leptospirosis is caused by the bacteria Leptospira, which can be found in the urine of infected animals, particularly rodents, and can contaminate water or soil.
- Symptoms in Humans: Symptoms range from mild flu-like symptoms to severe illness affecting the liver, kidneys, and nervous system.
- Prevention: Avoid contact with contaminated water, vaccinate pets, and control rodent populations around homes.

Reducing the Risk of Zoonotic Infections

1. Regular Veterinary Care

- Ensure pets receive regular check-ups and vaccinations. Routine veterinary care can identify and treat zoonotic diseases early.
- Keep pets' vaccinations up to date, particularly for diseases like rabies and leptospirosis.

2. Good Hygiene Practices

- Wash hands thoroughly with soap and water after handling pets, cleaning their living areas, and before eating.
- Clean and disinfect pet habitats, bedding, and litter boxes regularly.

3. Safe Handling of Pet Waste

- Use gloves when cleaning litter boxes or picking up pet waste. Dispose of waste properly.
- Avoid direct contact with pet feces and urine, and wash hands immediately after disposal.

4. Preventative Measures for Specific Pets

- For cats: Keep them indoors to reduce exposure to disease-carrying wildlife, and maintain a flea control program.
- For dogs: Avoid letting them drink from or swim in potentially contaminated water sources.
- For reptiles and amphibians: Avoid keeping these pets in households with young children, pregnant women, or immunocompromised individuals, as they are common carriers of Salmonella.

5. Education and Awareness

- Educate family members, especially children, about the importance of handwashing and safe handling of pets.
- Stay informed about the zoonotic diseases common in your area and the specific risks associated with your pets.

6. Food Safety

- Avoid feeding pets raw meat or eggs, which can carry harmful bacteria.
- Store pet food properly and dispose of uneaten food to prevent bacterial growth.

7. Control External Parasites

- Use veterinarian-recommended products to control fleas, ticks, and other external parasites that can transmit diseases.
- Regularly check pets for signs of parasites and treat infestations promptly.

8. Prompt Medical Attention

- Seek medical attention immediately if bitten or scratched by an animal, particularly if the animal's vaccination status is unknown.
- Consult a healthcare provider if you experience symptoms of a zoonotic disease, especially after contact with pets.

Pets enrich our lives in many ways, but they also come with responsibilities, including the need to prevent and manage zoonotic infections. By following good hygiene practices, ensuring regular veterinary care, and staying informed about the risks, pet owners can significantly reduce the chances of zoonotic disease transmission. A proactive approach to pet care not only safeguards human health but also promotes the well-being of our beloved animal companions, ensuring a safe and harmonious coexistence.

16

Care for your Dog During a Disaster

Natural disasters like cyclone, earthquakes, flood etc. can happen suddenly and put everyone, including our pets, in danger. Taking care of your dog during such situation means being prepared, staying calm and knowing what to do. This article provides simple steps to help you care for your dog during a disaster.

Before a Disaster make an emergency plan

i. Find Safe Spots: Identify safe places in your home and community where you can go with your dog.

ii. Know evacuation routes: Plan different ways to leave your home in case one way is blocked and find pet-friendly shelters in your area.

iii. Emergency Contacts: Keep a list of important contacts, such as your vet, local animal control, and pet-friendly hotels.

Prepare a pet emergency /first aid kit

An emergency kit for pet is a vital part of your overall disaster preparedness plan. It ensures that your pet has everything they need to stay safe, healthy, and comfortable during an emergency. By taking the time to assemble a comprehensive emergency kit, you can provide your pet with the best possible care in the most challenging situations.

An emergency kit can help keep your dog safe and it include

i. Food and Water: Pack at least a week's worth of dog food and water. Don't forget bowls and a can opener if needed.

ii. Medications: Include your dog's medications and instructions for giving them.

iii. First Aid Kit: Pack bandages, antiseptic wipes, tweezers, and a pet first aid guide.

iv. Identification: Make sure your dog has up-to-date ID tags and a microchip. Include a recent photo of your dog.

v. Leash and Collar: Pack extra leashes and collars, and a harness if your dog uses one.
vi. Comfort Items: Bring toys, blankets, and bedding that your dog likes.
vii. Sanitation Supplies: Pack waste bags, paper towels, and disinfectant.

Training and Familiarization

i. Crate Training: Get your dog used to being in a crate, as it might be needed for transport or temporary housing.
ii. Basic Commands: Teach your dog basic commands like sit, stay, and come, which can help manage them in stressful situations.

During the Disaster

i. Stay Calm and Reassuring
ii. Stay Calm: Dogs can sense your emotions, so staying calm can help keep your dog calm too.
iii. Comfort Your Dog: Talk to your dog in a soothing voice and pet them gently.

Follow Your Emergency Plan

i. Keep Your Dog Secure: Use a leash or crate to keep your dog safe and prevent them from running away.
ii. Evacuate Early: If told to evacuate, do so right away and take your dog with you.
iii. Shelter in Place: If you can't leave, find a safe spot in your home and stay there with your dog.

After the Disaster

Check Your Dog's Condition

i. Look for Injuries: Check your dog for cuts, bruises, or other injuries and get vet care if needed.
ii. Watch for Stress: Look for signs of stress like panting, shaking, or changes in behavior.

Get Back to Normal

i. Keep Routines: Try to stick to your dog's regular feeding and exercise schedule.
ii. Provide Comfort: Spend extra time with your dog to help them feel secure.

Address Emotional Needs

i. Create a Safe Space: Set up a quiet, comfy area where your dog can relax.

ii. Seek Help if Needed: If your dog is very stressed, talk to your vet or an animal behavior expert.

Taking care of your dog during disaster means being prepared, acting quickly and giving them lots of love/ attention afterward. By following these simple steps, you can help keep your dog safe and comfortable during tough times.

17

Vaccination Schedule for Dogs A Comprehensive Guide

Vaccination is one of the most effective ways to protect dogs from potentially life-threatening diseases. It plays a crucial role in controlling infectious diseases and helps maintain both individual and herd immunity. Timely and appropriate vaccination of dogs not only safeguards their health but also prevents the spread of diseases to other animals and even humans in some cases. This article provides a detailed vaccination schedule for different diseases of dogs, including core and non-core vaccines, and highlights the importance of adhering to a proper vaccination regimen.

Vaccination is categorized into two main types: **core vaccines** and **non-core vaccines**. Core vaccines are considered essential for all dogs, regardless of their lifestyle or environment, while non-core vaccines are given based on individual risk factors like geography, lifestyle, and exposure to certain environments.

Core Vaccines for Dogs

Core vaccines are recommended for every dog due to the severity of the diseases they protect against. These diseases are widespread, highly contagious, and often fatal. Vaccination against these pathogens is crucial to prevent both individual illness and outbreaks within the dog population. Some core vaccines are also legally required in many areas, such as the rabies vaccine.

Non-Core Vaccines for Dogs

Non-core vaccines are not required for all dogs but are recommended based on individual risk factors, such as geographical location, lifestyle, or the likelihood of exposure to specific pathogens. Dogs that live in areas where certain diseases are prevalent or that frequently interact with other dogs in high-risk environments (boarding kennels, dog parks, etc.) may benefit from these vaccines.

Differences Between Core and Non-Core Vaccines

Aspect	Core Vaccines	Non-Core Vaccines
Necessity	Essential for all dogs.	Optional, based on individual risk factors.
Target Diseases	Widespread, severe, and often fatal diseases.	Diseases that affect specific regions or lifestyles.
Legal Requirements	Rabies is often legally required.	Generally not required by law.
Administration	Administered to all dogs regardless of lifestyle.	Administered based on exposure risks.

1. Core Vaccines

Core vaccines are considered essential for all dogs, regardless of their lifestyle or geographical location, due to the widespread nature of the diseases they prevent. These vaccines protect against severe and highly contagious diseases that pose a significant risk to both dogs and humans.

a. **Canine Distemper Virus (CDV):** Canine distemper is a highly contagious viral disease that affects the respiratory, gastrointestinal, and nervous systems.
   - Symptoms: Fever, nasal discharge, coughing, lethargy, vomiting, diarrhea, and neurological signs (seizures, paralysis).
   - Vaccination Schedule:
   - Puppies: First dose at 6–8 weeks, followed by booster doses every 3–4 weeks until 16 weeks of age.
   - Adults: Booster at one year, then every 1–3 years depending on the vaccine brand and the dog's risk level.

b. **Canine Parvovirus (CPV):** Canine parvovirus is a highly contagious virus that affects the gastrointestinal tract, leading to severe illness, especially in puppies.
   - Symptoms: Vomiting, bloody diarrhea, fever, lethargy, rapid dehydration, and weight loss.
   - Vaccination Schedule:
   - Puppies: First dose at 6–8 weeks, followed by booster doses every 3–4 weeks until 16 weeks of age.
   - Adults: Booster at one year, then every 1–3 years.

c. **Canine Adenovirus Type 2 (CAV-2):** Canine adenovirus type 2 causes respiratory infections (kennel cough) and protects against canine hepatitis caused by adenovirus type 1.

- Symptoms: Coughing, sneezing, nasal discharge, fever, and potentially liver failure in severe cases (CAV-1).
- Vaccination Schedule:
- Puppies: First dose at 6–8 weeks, followed by booster doses every 3–4 weeks until 16 weeks of age.
- Adults: Booster at one year, then every 1–3 years.

d. **Rabies Virus:** Rabies is a fatal viral disease that affects the central nervous system of mammals, including dogs and humans. It is zoonotic and transmitted through bites.
  - Symptoms: Behavioral changes, aggression, excessive drooling, paralysis, and eventually death.
  - Vaccination Schedule:
  - Puppies: First dose at 12–16 weeks of age.
  - Adults: Booster at one year, then every 1–3 years as required by local regulations.

2. Non-Core Vaccines

Non-core vaccines are recommended based on a dog's individual risk factors such as lifestyle, geographical location, and exposure to certain environments (e.g., boarding kennels, dog parks). These vaccines are important for dogs with increased risk of exposure to specific diseases.

a. **Bordetella bronchiseptica (Kennel Cough):** Bordetella is a bacterial infection that is a primary cause of kennel cough, a highly contagious respiratory illness.
  - Symptoms: Coughing, retching, nasal discharge, and sometimes fever.
  - Vaccination Schedule:
  - Puppies: First dose at 8–12 weeks of age.
  - Adults: Booster annually or more frequently (every 6 months) for dogs in high-risk environments such as boarding facilities.

b. **Leptospirosis:** Leptospirosis is a bacterial infection that can affect dogs and humans (zoonotic). It can cause kidney and liver damage.
  - Symptoms: Fever, vomiting, diarrhea, muscle pain, lethargy, and jaundice.
  - Vaccination Schedule:
  - Puppies: First dose at 12 weeks of age, followed by a booster 3–4 weeks later.

- Adults: Booster annually, especially for dogs in high-risk areas or with exposure to wildlife and standing water.

c. **Lyme Disease (Borrelia burgdorferi)**: Lyme disease is caused by a bacterium transmitted through tick bites and can lead to joint inflammation, fever, and kidney disease.

- Symptoms: Fever, limping, swelling of the joints, lethargy, and loss of appetite.
- Vaccination Schedule:
- Puppies: First dose at 12 weeks of age, followed by a booster 3–4 weeks later.
- Adults: Annual boosters for dogs in high-risk areas where tick exposure is common.

d. **Canine Influenza Virus (CIV)**: Canine influenza is a contagious respiratory disease caused by strains of influenza viruses.

- Symptoms: Cough, runny nose, fever, lethargy, and reduced appetite.
- Vaccination Schedule:
- Puppies: First dose at 6–8 weeks of age, followed by a booster 3–4 weeks later.
- Adults: Annual boosters, particularly for dogs frequently exposed to other dogs in kennels, shelters, or dog shows.

Puppy Vaccination Schedule Overview

Age (Weeks)	Vaccines
6–8	Distemper, Parvovirus, Adenovirus-2 (DA2P), Bordetella (optional)
10–12	DA2P, Bordetella (optional), Leptospirosis (optional)
12–16	DA2P, Rabies, Bordetella (optional), Leptospirosis (optional), Lyme (optional)
16	Rabies (if not given earlier), final DA2P booster

Adult Dog Vaccination Schedule Overview

Once a dog has completed the initial puppy series, adult dogs generally follow an annual or triennial vaccination schedule, depending on the specific vaccine and the dog's risk factors. Some core vaccines like rabies and DA2P are administered every 1–3 years, while non-core vaccines like leptospirosis, Bordetella, and Lyme disease may require annual boosters.

Vaccine	Adult Dog Schedule
Rabies	Every 1–3 years
Distemper (DA2P)	Every 1–3 years

Vaccine	Adult Dog Schedule
Parvovirus (DA2P)	Every 1–3 years
Adenovirus-2 (DA2P)	Every 1–3 years
Bordetella	Every 6–12 months (if at risk)
Leptospirosis	Annual booster (if at risk)
Lyme Disease	Annual booster (if at risk)
Canine Influenza	Annual booster (if at risk)

Considerations for Special Cases

Pregnant Dogs: Avoid live vaccines, such as the modified live virus (MLV) distemper vaccine, in pregnant dogs as these could potentially affect the unborn puppies.

Senior Dogs: Older dogs may have a lower risk of contracting certain diseases, and veterinarians may tailor their vaccination schedules accordingly. However, annual or triennial vaccines are often still recommended to maintain immunity.

Dogs with Pre-existing Health Conditions: Dogs with chronic health conditions or weakened immune systems may require special vaccination schedules or may be recommended to avoid certain vaccines.

Potential Side Effects of Vaccinations: While vaccines are generally safe, mild side effects can occur in some dogs. These can include:

- Mild fever
- Lethargy
- Swelling or soreness at the injection site
- Allergic reactions (rare but serious) such as facial swelling, difficulty breathing, or vomiting

It's important to monitor your dog after vaccination and contact your veterinarian if any concerning symptoms arise.

Importance of Veterinary Consultation

Always consult with your veterinarian to determine the best vaccination schedule for your dog. Factors such as geographic location, lifestyle, age, and underlying health conditions will influence the recommendations for both core and non-core vaccines.

In conclusion, a well-structured vaccination schedule is essential for protecting your dog from various infectious diseases. Core vaccines are vital for all dogs, while non-core vaccines should be administered based on the dog's risk of exposure. By following the recommended vaccination schedule, you ensure that your dog remains healthy and protected throughout their life.

18

Nutritional Guide for Pet Dogs of Different Age Groups

Proper nutrition is essential for the health and well-being of dogs at every stage of life. The nutritional needs of a dog change as it grows, so it's important to tailor their diet according to their age, size, and health status. Below is a comprehensive guide on the nutritional needs of dogs, broken down into different age groups: puppies, adult dogs, and senior dogs.

1. Puppies (0-12 Months)

Puppies are in a rapid growth phase and require a high level of nutrients, including proteins, fats, vitamins, and minerals, to support the development of muscles, bones, organs, and the immune system.

Nutritional Needs

Protein: Puppies require high-quality animal-based protein to build muscle and tissue. Around 22-30% of their diet should be protein-rich. Chicken, turkey, fish, and eggs are excellent sources.

Fats: Fats provide a concentrated source of energy for growing puppies. Essential fatty acids like omega-3 and omega-6 are crucial for brain development, healthy skin, and coat. Fat content should be around 10-25%.

Carbohydrates: Puppies can also benefit from carbohydrates, which provide energy and help with digestion. Whole grains, like brown rice and oatmeal, and vegetables, like sweet potatoes and carrots, are ideal.

Calcium and Phosphorus: These minerals are vital for bone development. Growing puppies need a balanced intake of calcium and phosphorus, generally in a 1.2:1 ratio, to prevent skeletal issues like hip dysplasia.

Vitamins and Minerals: Puppies require a wide range of vitamins and minerals, including vitamins A, D, E, and B-complex, for overall development and immune health.

Feeding Schedule

0-6 weeks: Puppies should nurse from their mother or be fed a high-quality puppy milk replacer. No solid food should be introduced until around 4 weeks.

6-12 weeks: Start with a balanced puppy formula and introduce solid food gradually. Puppies should be fed 3-4 times a day.

3-6 months: Continue feeding high-quality puppy food, but reduce feeding to 3 times a day.

6-12 months: Begin transitioning to an adult dog food. Depending on the breed, large-breed puppies may take longer to fully mature.

Special Considerations

Large-breed puppies**: Need controlled calcium intake to prevent rapid growth that can stress bones and joints. Consider large-breed-specific puppy formulas.

Small-breed puppies**: They have higher metabolic rates and may need more frequent meals with nutrient-dense foods.

2. Adult Dogs (1-7 Years)

As dogs reach adulthood, their growth slows, and they enter a maintenance phase. Their diet should be well-balanced and designed to maintain energy levels, muscle mass, and overall health without leading to obesity.

Nutritional Needs

Protein: Adult dogs still need high-quality protein, though less than puppies. A diet with 18-25% protein is generally sufficient, depending on the breed and activity level.

Fats: Fats are important for energy, but overfeeding fats can lead to weight gain in less active dogs. Fat content should be about 10-15%.

Carbohydrates: Adult dogs benefit from digestible carbohydrates for energy. Whole grains, fruits, and vegetables provide fiber and are a good source of vitamins.

Vitamins and Minerals: A balance of essential vitamins (A, E, D, B-complex) and minerals (calcium, phosphorus, potassium) supports immune function, skin health, and bone strength.

Water: Clean and fresh water is critical to maintain proper hydration and digestion.

Feeding Schedule

Adult dogs should be fed 1-2 times a day. The amount depends on their size, activity level, and breed.

Special Considerations

Active Dogs: Working dogs or those that engage in high levels of activity may need higher caloric intake, particularly from proteins and fats.

Small Breeds: Small dogs have faster metabolisms and may need smaller, more frequent meals.

Large Breeds: Large dogs are more prone to weight gain and joint problems, so lower-calorie formulas are often beneficial.

3. Senior Dogs (7+ Years)

As dogs age, their metabolism slows down, and they become more susceptible to age-related health problems such as arthritis, obesity, and dental issues. A well-managed diet can help mitigate these problems and extend the dog's life quality.

Nutritional Needs

Protein: Senior dogs need high-quality protein to maintain muscle mass and support organ function. Diets with around 20% protein are suitable for most senior dogs. The protein source should be easily digestible (e.g., chicken, fish).

Fats: Fat intake should be moderated as senior dogs tend to be less active. A fat content of around 8-12% is recommended to avoid weight gain.

Carbohydrates: Fiber is important for promoting digestion and preventing constipation in older dogs. Sources such as sweet potatoes, oatmeal, and brown rice are ideal.

Vitamins and Minerals: Senior dogs often require supplements of vitamins and minerals such as glucosamine and chondroitin for joint support, antioxidants like vitamin E for immune health, and omega-3 fatty acids for anti-inflammatory effects.

Low Phosphorus: For older dogs, especially those with kidney problems, it's important to lower phosphorus intake to protect kidney function.

Feeding Schedule

Senior dogs should be fed 1-2 times daily with consideration for their slower metabolism. Some may benefit from smaller, more frequent meals if they have digestive issues.

Special Considerations

Weight Management: Senior dogs are prone to weight gain due to reduced activity. Opt for senior dog food with lower calories.

Joint Health: Foods or supplements with glucosamine and chondroitin can help maintain joint health and mobility.

Dental Health: Softened foods or specially formulated kibble may help dogs with dental issues.

4. Tailoring Nutrition Based on Breed and Size

Small-Breed Dogs: Small dogs often require diets with higher calorie densities due to their fast metabolism. They also benefit from foods that are easier to chew and digest.

Large-Breed Dogs: Large-breed dogs are more prone to joint issues and obesity. They benefit from lower-calorie diets that provide joint support through ingredients like glucosamine and chondroitin.

Working and Sporting Dogs: These dogs need diets rich in fats and proteins to sustain their high energy output. Specialized formulas are designed to meet the demands of these breeds.

5. Homemade Diets and Supplements

While commercial dog food is often nutritionally balanced, some pet owners prefer to prepare homemade diets. If considering this option, it's important to ensure the dog's diet contains all essential nutrients. Consultation with a veterinarian or pet nutritionist is advised. Essential supplements may include:

- Calcium: If feeding a homemade diet, ensure adequate calcium is provided.
- Omega-3 Fatty Acids: To support skin, coat, and brain health.
- Probiotics: To aid digestion and improve gut health.
- Multivitamins: For balanced micronutrient intake, especially in senior dogs.

Feeding your dog according to its life stage and specific needs is crucial for maintaining their health, longevity, and quality of life. Always ensure that the diet you choose is balanced, providing appropriate protein, fats, carbohydrates, vitamins, and minerals. Tailor their food intake based on their age, breed, size, and lifestyle, and adjust as needed throughout their lifetime. When in doubt, always consult with a veterinarian for guidance.

Index

B
Beagle 1, 13
Behavior 24, 33, 34, 35

C
Canine Distemper 23, 70

D
Dachshund 13, 14
Disaster 65, 66, 67
Diseases 17, 23, 24, 28, 61, 63, 64, 69, 70, 71, 73

E
Eye and Ear Care 31, 32

F
Fleas and Ticks 19, 24, 28

G
Grooming 1, 14, 17, 19, 21, 27, 34, 45, 51, 57, 60

H
Heartworm Disease 24
Hygiene 21, 24, 34, 41, 42, 43, 57, 59, 60, 62, 63, 64

O
Obesity 24, 37, 38, 49, 76, 77, 78
Oral Care 41, 43

P
Pariah Dog 1, 13
Parvovirus 23, 70
Pomeranian 13
Pregnancy 53, 54, 56

R
Rabies 23, 24, 45, 61, 63, 69, 71, 72
Retriever 1, 13, 38

S
Senior Dogs 34, 49, 50, 51, 73, 75, 77, 78
Skin Care 27, 29
Springtime 19, 20
Summer 15, 16, 17, 39, 50

T
Travel 45, 46, 47

W
Whelping 53, 54, 55, 56
Winter 19, 21, 22, 50

Z
Zoonotic Infections 61, 63, 64